I0797543

Lerner SPORTS

SPORTS ALL-STARS

CHRISTIAN YELICH

Jon M. Fishman

Lerner Publications ◆ Minneapolis

SCORE BIG with sports fans, reluctant readers, and report writers!

Lerner Sports is a database of high-interest biographies profiling notable sports superstars. Packed with fascinating facts, these bios explore the backgrounds, career-defining moments, and everyday lives of popular athletes. Lerner Sports is perfect for young readers developing research skills or looking for exciting sports content.

LERNER SPORTS FEATURES:

- Keyword search
- Topic navigation menus
- Fast facts
- Related bio suggestions to encourage more reading
- Admin view of reader statistics
- Fresh content updated regularly

and more!

Visit LernerSports.com for a free trial!

Copyright © 2020 by Lerner Publishing Group, Inc.

All rights reserved. International copyright secured. No part of this book may be reproduced, stored in a retrieval system, or transmitted in any form or by any means—electronic, mechanical, photocopying, recording, or otherwise—without the prior written permission of Lerner Publishing Group, Inc., except for the inclusion of brief quotations in an acknowledged review.

Lerner Publications Company
An imprint of Lerner Publishing Group, Inc.
241 First Avenue North
Minneapolis, MN 55401 USA

For reading levels and more information, look up this title at www.lernerbooks.com.

Main body text set in Albany Std. Typeface provided by Agfa.

Library of Congress Cataloging-in-Publication Data

Names: Fishman, Jon M., author. | Lerner Publications Company.
Title: Christian Yelich / Jon M. Fishman.
Other titles: Sports all-stars (Lerner Publications Company)
Description: Minneapolis : Lerner Publications, 2020. | Series: Sports all-stars (Lerner Sports) | Includes bibliographical references and index. | Audience: Ages 7–11 years | Audience: Grades 2–3 | Summary: "Outfielder Christian Yelich joined the Milwaukee Brewers in 2018 and won the National League Most Valuable Player award. Follow Yelich's rise to baseball superstardom"— Provided by publisher.
Identifiers: LCCN 2019030963 (print) | LCCN 2019030964 (ebook) | ISBN 9781541597907 (Library Binding) | ISBN 9781541597914 (Paperback) | ISBN 9781541597921 (eBook)
Subjects: LCSH: Yelich, Christian, 1991—Juvenile literature. | Outfielders (Baseball)—United States—Biography. | Baseball players—United States—Biography. | Milwaukee Brewers (Baseball team)—History. | Major League Baseball (Organization)—History.
Classification: LCC GV865.Y43 F57 2020 (print) | LCC GV865.Y43 (ebook) | DDC 796.357092 [B]—dc23

LC record available at https://lccn.loc.gov/2019030963
LC ebook record available at https://lccn.loc.gov/2019030964

Manufactured in the United States of America
1-47979-48405-9/18/2019

CONTENTS

POWER BREWER

Yelich readies a powerful swing in June 2019.

On Opening Day of the 2019 Major League Baseball (MLB) season, some fans probably still doubted Milwaukee Brewers outfielder Christian Yelich.

FACTS AT A GLANCE

- **Date of Birth:** December 5, 1991
- **Position:** outfielder
- **League:** MLB
- **Professional Highlights:** was traded to the Milwaukee Brewers in 2018; helped Milwaukee reach the 2018 National League (NL) Championship series; won the 2018 NL Most Valuable Player (MVP) award
- **Personal Highlights:** grew up in Thousand Oaks, California; has two younger brothers, Collin and Cameron; his great-grandfather received an award from the Pro Football Hall of Fame

He had been a good hitter for the Miami Marlins during the first five seasons of his career. But he hadn't been great. Then, in his first season with the Brewers, he started playing better than ever and won the 2018 NL MVP award. He couldn't be that good again in 2019. Could he?

It didn't take long for Yelich to destroy any doubts about his baseball skills. By the middle of the 2019 season, he ranked in the NL's top five in **batting average**, runs, and **stolen bases**. He also smashed home run after home run. When the Brewers faced the Houston Astros on June 11, Yelich's 24 home runs were the most in the NL.

Yelich hit a **double** to center field in the first inning against Houston. A few batters later, he raced home to score the first run of the game. Brewers 1, Astros 0.

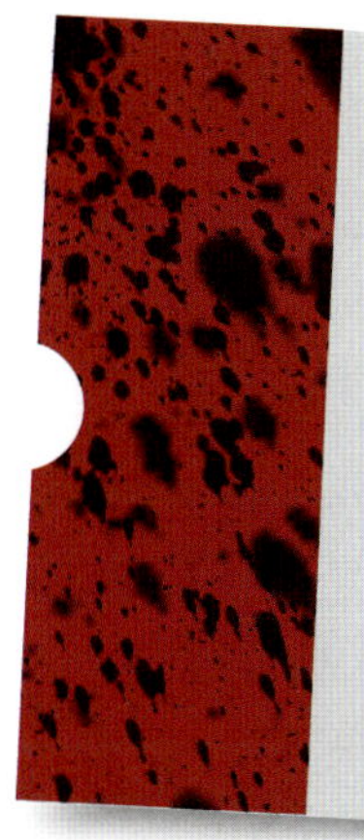

The Brewers started out as the Seattle Pilots. The team moved to Milwaukee and changed their name in 1970.

When Yelich came to bat in the third inning, Houston held a 2–1 lead. Astros pitcher Brad Peacock was cautious. He didn't want to throw a pitch over the middle of home plate where Yelich could crush it. He threw a strike and then three **balls** in a row. One more ball and Yelich would take first base.

Peacock had to throw a strike. The pitch soared over the middle of the plate at the perfect height for Yelich. He lifted his front leg and stepped forward as he swung. *Crack!* The ball rocketed off his bat and over the right field wall for a home run.

The home run was Yelich's 25th of the season. No Brewers player had ever hit 25 home runs so quickly. Though Houston won that game 10–8, Yelich has a lot to celebrate. With his smooth, powerful swing, he could become the best home run hitter in Brewers history.

BASEBALL BOY

Yelich practices with the Marlins in 2013.

Christian Yelich might have been a football player. He was born on December 5, 1991, to a family with a rich football history. His great-grandfather, Fred Gehrke, played for the National Football League's Los Angeles Rams

Fred Gehrke painted the curved horn on his helmet when he played for the Rams.

in the 1940s. Gehrke created the curved-horn helmet design that the Rams still use. In 1972, he received a special award from the Pro Football Hall of Fame for his design. Chris Yelich, Christian's uncle, played football for the University of California, Los Angeles, in the 1980s.

But Christian fell in love with baseball as a kid. He grew up in Thousand Oaks, California. Since many former MLB players came from the area, he had plenty of baseball role models. Besides, Christian's friends played baseball, so he did too.

Christian in high school, when he played first base

Christian has two younger brothers, Collin and Cameron. Like Christian, Collin loves baseball. The two boys played Wiffle ball together for hours at a time in their yard. "We grew as brothers through the game of baseball," Collin said. "That's all we did as kids was play baseball."

Christian joined Little League when he was about seven years old. When he was older, he played on youth travel teams. Most travel teams practice all year. During the season, they go to other cities and states to play games. Travel-team baseball was a big commitment for Christian and his family. He missed birthday parties and nights with his friends. But that was okay with him. Christian loved baseball and took the sport seriously.

Christian's talent and commitment showed on the field. He played on Westlake High School's **varsity** team as a freshman. He had a .373 batting average in 25 games. It was a good start to an incredible high school career. By his senior year, **scouts** ranked him as the 30th best

Yelich's brother Cameron (*left*) once threw the first pitch of the game.

high school player in the United States. That season he batted .451 and scored 41 runs in 28 games.

In June 2010, the Marlins chose Yelich with the 23rd overall pick in the MLB draft. He was thrilled that Miami took him so early. "I knew they had interest, but not this kind of interest," he said. "It's definitely a welcome surprise." Next, he would have to prove himself in the **minor leagues**.

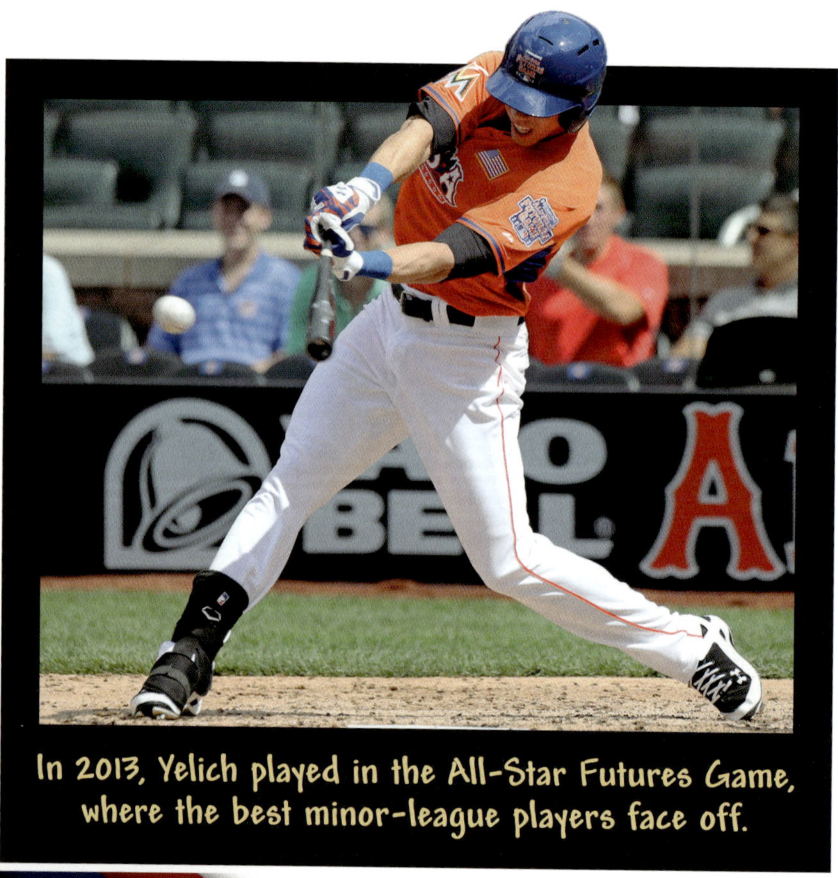

In 2013, Yelich played in the All-Star Futures Game, where the best minor-league players face off.

ALWAYS WORKING

Yelich trains to keep his skills sharp and his body strong.

Yelich sweats as he hangs from a metal bar in a gym. A heavy chain loops around his neck, weighing him down. He pulls himself up until his chin is even with the bar before relaxing his arms. Then he pulls himself up again.

Yelich practices batting during spring training with the Brewers.

Yelich's commitment to fitness and exercise is one reason the Marlins chose him in the draft. In high school, he worked out at Proactive Sports Performance in California. The training center designs special workouts for athletes to reach different goals. In 2014, Yelich restarted his training at Proactive during baseball's **off-season**. He works out to prepare his body for MLB's tough 162-game schedule.

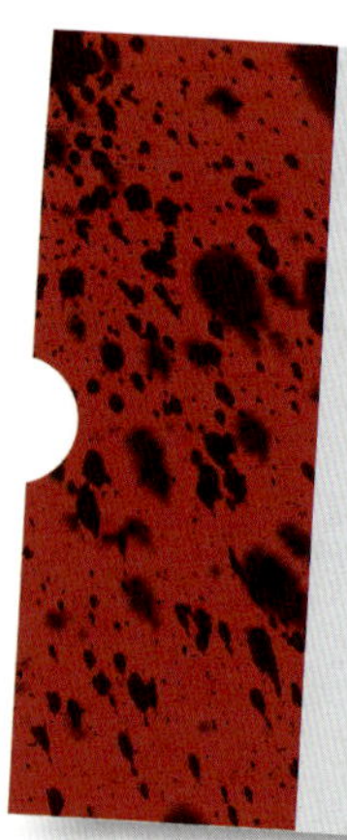

The Brewers have a chef who prepares healthful meals for the players. When Yelich eats with his family, they often have his favorite food: tacos.

Yelich focuses on different regions of his body on different days. On leg days, he moves heavy weights without using his arms. He may use machines specially designed for leg workouts. Or he might push a heavy cart across the floor. He does many different exercises to target all the muscles in his legs. Other days, he focuses on strengthening his arms, stomach, or back.

In spring training, Yelich works on improving his baseball skills.

Yelich often exercises with **resistance bands**. He may strap the bands around his legs or hips to make movements tougher. The bands provide a good workout and cause less stress to the body than heavy weights do.

Yelich uses resistance bands to stretch and warm up before games.

Friendly competition motivates Yelich during training.

One way Yelich motivates himself is by competing with workout buddies. He might race a friend to see who can complete an exercise faster. Working out with friends helps make time in the gym fun.

Yelich and teammate Lorenzo Cain arrive at the field for a workout in 2018.

During the MLB season, teams play almost every day. That doesn't leave a lot of time for gym workouts. In the years he played for the Marlins, Yelich didn't work out during the season. That changed in 2018. He spent time in the gym all season to maintain his strength. It was one reason he stayed strong until the final game and won the NL MVP award.

MVP LIFE

After winning the NL MVP award, Yelich spent the winter of 2019 touring the United States to speak about baseball.

In January 2019, Yelich stepped onstage at the New York Hilton Midtown Manhattan Hotel wearing a black suit and a bow tie. He was at a formal dinner to receive his MVP award for the 2018 season.

Yelich signs a jersey for fans in 2018.

With fellow players and cameras watching, Yelich spoke into the microphone. "What a year it's been," he said.

The event was one stop on Yelich's winter trip. He traveled around the country doing interviews and going to awards shows. He wanted to attract more fans to the sport he loved. "Obviously you want to bring as much attention to the game as possible and grow baseball as much as you can," he said. "It's important."

Beach House

When he isn't traveling during the off-season, Yelich spends time at home in Malibu, California. He bought a house in the city near Las Flores Beach in 2018. The $5.6 million home has elevators, a firepit on the roof, and amazing views of the Pacific Ocean.

Las Flores Beach

Being near the beach is important to Yelich. He spent a lot of time on Malibu's beaches with his family as a kid. In 2019, he helped Louisville Slugger create a special bat. Yelich's design includes beach colors, waves, and a lifeguard tower.

Fire approaches Malibu homes in November 2018.

In November 2018, wildfires raged around Malibu, in Southern California. The fires destroyed hundreds of buildings and did billions of dollars in damage. Many people fled their homes for safety, including Yelich and teammate Ryan Braun.

Yelich, some teammates, and Rams quarterback Jared Goff started California Strong to help victims of the disasters in Southern California. In 2019, they hosted a special softball game in Malibu. The game raised money for California Strong. With Yelich's efforts, the group has raised more than $1 million to help victims get hotels, fill their gas tanks, and replace their personal items.

From left: Mike Moustakas, Yelich, Mike Attanasio, and Ryan Braun at the California Strong softball game

ON THE MOVE

Yelich at bat for the Marlins

Yelich spent almost four seasons in the minor leagues before playing his first MLB game. He played for teams such as the Jupiter Hammerheads and the Greensboro Grasshoppers. He worked on his skills and moved up through the minor leagues as he improved.

Yelich slides into third base.

Yelich's first MLB game came in the middle of the 2013 season. On July 23, the Marlins called him up to face the Colorado Rockies. He smacked a hit in the third inning to help a teammate score and tie the game. He finished with two hits in Miami's 4–2 win.

It was a good start to Yelich's career. But during his time in Florida, the Marlins lost more often than they won. Yelich and superstar Giancarlo Stanton weren't enough to make Miami a playoff team. In December 2017, the

Yelich (*left*) and Giancarlo Stanton played together with the Marlins.

Marlins traded Stanton to the New York Yankees. About two months later, they sent Yelich to the Brewers. He welcomed the move.

In his first year with Milwaukee, Yelich set career-high marks in batting average, home runs, stolen bases, and runs. He helped the Brewers reach the NL Championship Series before they lost to the Los Angeles Dodgers. Milwaukee fans hope Yelich can lead the team to the World Series.

Yelich slams a hit for the Brewers in 2019.

Batting Average

Christian Yelich	.326
Scooter Gennett	.310
Freddie Freeman	.309
Anthony Rendon	.308
Lorenzo Cain	.308

Home Runs

Nolan Arenado	38
Trevor Story	37
Christian Yelich	36
Matt Carpenter	36
Jesus Aguilar	35
Max Muncy	35

Runs

Charlie Blackmon	119
Christian Yelich	118
Matt Carpenter	111
Ozzie Albies	105
Nolan Arenado	104

Source Notes

10 Clark Spencer, "From Wiffle Ball to Marlins Camp, Yelich Brothers Together Again," *Miami Herald*, March 23, 2017, https://www.miamiherald.com/sports/spt-columns-blogs/fish-bytes/article140435718.html.

12 Matt Blue, "Scouting Florida Marlins 2010: First Round Draft Pick Christian Yelich," Bleacher Report, July 21, 2010, https://bleacherreport.com/articles/423301-scouting-florida-marlins-2010-first-round-draft-pick-christian-yelich.

20 Greg Hill, "Christian Yelich Accepts His MVP Award," *WTMJ*, January 26, 2019, http://www.wtmj.com/sports/baseball/milwaukee-brewers/christian-yelich-accepts-his-mvp-award/991149769.

20 Tyler Kepner and James Wagner, "Christian Yelich on Life as an M.V.P. and Why He Never Guesses at the Plate," *New York Times*, January 28, 2019, https://www.nytimes.com/2019/01/28/sports/baseball/christian-yelich-milwaukee-brewers.html.

Glossary

balls: pitches that miss the strike zone

batting average: the ratio of a batter's hits per times at bat

double: a base hit that allows the batter to reach second base

minor leagues: baseball leagues where players train and prepare for MLB

off-season: the part of a year when a sports league is inactive

resistance bands: straps that stretch and provide resistance during workouts

scouts: people who judge the skills of athletes

stolen bases: when base runners advance to bases they aren't entitled to, usually as pitchers throw to home plate

varsity: the top team at a school

Further Information

California Strong
https://www.californiastrong.org/

Fishman, Jon M. *Giancarlo Stanton.* Minneapolis: Lerner Publications, 2019.

Kelley, K. C. *Milwaukee Brewers.* Mankato, MN: Child's World, 2019.

MLB
https://www.mlb.com/

Official Site of the Milwaukee Brewers
https://www.mlb.com/brewers

Seidel, Jeff. *Pro Baseball Upsets.* Minneapolis: Lerner Publications, 2020.

Index

Photo Acknowledgments

Image credits: Tim Warner/Getty Images, pp. 4, 6; Joe Rimkus Jr./Miami Herald/Tribune News Service/Getty Images, p. 8; Rich Graessle/Icon Sportswire/Getty Images, p. 9; Gary Friedman/Los Angeles Times/Getty Images, p. 10; Stacy Revere/Getty Images, p. 11; Tim Clayton/MLB/Getty Images, p. 12; Joel Auerbach/Getty Images, pp. 13, 16; Will Powers/Icon Sportswire/Getty Images, pp. 14, 17; Alex Trautwig/MLB/Getty Images, pp. 15, 18, 19; Adam Glanzman/MLB /Getty Images, p. 20; Cedric Parsiegla/EyeEm/Getty Images, p. 21; David McNew/Getty Images, p. 22; Rich Polk/Getty Images, p. 23; Dustin Bradford/Getty Images, pp. 24, 25; Paul Bereswill/Getty Images, p. 26; Scott Taetsch//Getty Images, p. 27.

Cover: Quinn Harris/Getty Images.